IMAGES
of America

NORTHERN
VIRGINIA'S
EQUESTRIAN HERITAGE

The caption for this group of photos in a 1931 copy of *Loudoun-Faquier Breeders* magazine reads "Upper left: Miss Bettina Belmont, daughter of Mrs. Arthur White, taking one of the jumps on Cedarbrook. Upper right: The third race at the Burrland Race Meet. Center: Mrs. John Hay Whitney, on Number 4, rides winner in Ladies' Race on Ziegler Estate. Lower left: Mr. and Mrs. William Ziegler, Jr., on whose estate the meet was held. Lower center: Mr. and Mrs. John Hay Whitney watching their horses perform. Lower right: Miss Ann Leith with Bandit Flag, on which she won the hunter trials."

IMAGES
of America

NORTHERN
VIRGINIA'S
EQUESTRIAN HERITAGE

Mary L. Fishback

ARCADIA
PUBLISHING

Published by Arcadia Publishing
Charleston, South Carolina

Printed in the United States of America

Library of Congress Catalog Card Number: 200109868

For all general information contact Arcadia Publishing at:
Telephone 843-853-2070
Fax 843-853-0044
E-Mail sales@arcadiapublishing.com
For customer service and orders:
Toll-Free 1-888-313-2665

Visit us on the Internet at www.arcadiapublishing.com

This book is dedicated to the horses, the riders, and the impact the equine culture has had on Northern Virginia over the past 100 years.

CONTENTS

The caption for this group of photographs in a 1930 copy of *Loudoun-Faquier Breeders* magazine reads "(a) Part of the crowd at the Warrenton races gathered about the Paddock, viewing the horses and riders before the first race. (b) William Almy, Jr. up on Skyscraper taking a nose dive over the first jump of the course. (c) Seraglio with Jockey William B. Street up, owned by Mrs. John Hay Whitney, Jr., crossing the finish line, winner by a large margin. (d) William B. Street, rider of Seraglio, owned by Mrs. John Hay Whitney, Jr., about to receive the cup, held by Mrs. Whitney and presented by Mrs. Baldwin Spilman, Jr., on whose estate the race was run. (e) Dave O'Dell who was up on Our Way and finished third in the Canterbury Cup. (f) Harry J. Duffy, Jr., who was up on So Dear and finished third, chatting informally over the Paddock fence, with Miss Jean McClure of New York."

INTRODUCTION

This pictorial volume aims to introduce readers to the earlier days of equestrian life in the Northern Virginia area. I chose three collections of photographs to best illustrate how all forms of equestrian sports have influenced Northern Virginia.

The first, Morven Park, which was the home of two governors, Thomas Swann of Maryland and Westmoreland Davis of Virginia, is internationally known in the field of equine medicine through the Marion duPont Equine Center. Morven Park is also the location of the Museum of Hounds and Hunting.

The second is from the magazine *The Chronicle of the Horse*, located in Middleburg, Virginia, and founded in the 1930s, which is dedicated to all forms of local, national, and international horsemanship. Their archives house one the best photographic histories of horses and hounds that I have ever seen.

The third collection is from the National Sporting Library in Middleburg, Virginia. This library is dedicated to the preservation of some of the most rare manuscripts and art works in the world. Its archives are vast and cover thousands of topics that relate to hunting, racing, jumping, and all types of equestrian events as well as field sports and other related subjects.

In these photographs, readers will witness a part of history rarely, if ever, seen in print. The photos are of the famous and infamous and how they lived. Images reveal how and why hunts evolved; unusual pictures of homes and properties related to this pastime are also included. These three collections, plus a section on Loudoun County's own contributions to equestrian heritage, combine to offer a fascinating look at a treasured part of Northern Virginia's history.

Nancy Lee Burnest painted *Tom Taylor's Horse* in 1954. (Courtesy Winslow Williams Collection, Balch Library.)

One

THE MYSTIQUE OF MORVEN PARK

Nestled in the lush Loudoun countryside is the elegant estate of Morven Park, which comprises 1,200 acres and includes a large manor house that was built around 1781. Once owned by Dr. Wilson C. Seldon, the property was sold to Gov. Thomas Swann of Maryland, who promptly set about expanding the house. In 1903, Virginia Gov. Westmoreland Davis and his wife, Marguerite Grace Inman, acquired the estate.

Upon obtaining the property, Governor Davis began to transform Morven Park into an agricultural show place. He immersed himself in scientific farming, building extensive barns, carriage houses, green houses, and buildings for breeding horses, turkey, hogs, sheep, and dairy stock. He planted the most progressive crops in the area and practiced crop rotation.

In 1912, Governor Davis was president and publisher of the magazine Southern Planter. An avid equestrian and foxhunter, as well as a bird and large game hunter, Governor Davis was renowned for his large parties at Morven Park, which accommodated 600 or more guests at a time. In 1909, he was chairman of the Hunts Committee of the National Steeplechase and Hunt Association.

Governor Davis lived at Morven Park during his term as governor of Virginia. The manor house at Morven reflects his varied and organized lifestyle. From the lions at the entrance, to the Flemish Brabant tapestries that adorn the main hall, to the richly wooded game room with its trophies, one can actually get a feel for Westmoreland Davis. The home takes visitors back to the grand era of Virginia's stately manor houses.

Today the Morven Park mansion is open to the public through the generosity of the Westmoreland Davis Memorial Foundation Inc. established by Marguerite Inman Davis.

As this artist's rendition shows, not all of the lavish plans for Morven Park materialized while under the ownership of Gov. Thomas Swann.

Gov. Westmoreland Davis and his wife, Marguerite, enjoyed casual rides on their beautiful estate, Morven Park. (Courtesy Morven Park Archives.)

This photo shows the southeast end of the green house that was the pride of Governor Davis. In it, he grew beautiful flowers, exotic plants, and kept seedlings for trees and shrubs. Since his ownership, it has been restored and additions have been made. There are lovely outdoor planting beds, ornate boxwood gardens, and old magnolia trees scattered about the estate. (Author photo.)

Governor and Mrs. Davis were accomplished equestrians. They both rode in hunts and enjoyed their animals. The Davises later acquired another large estate, Big Spring, located just north of Leesburg. There they built these attractive brick stables for their horses. These stables remain much the same today, even though Big Spring has been subdivided. (Courtesy Morven Park Archives.)

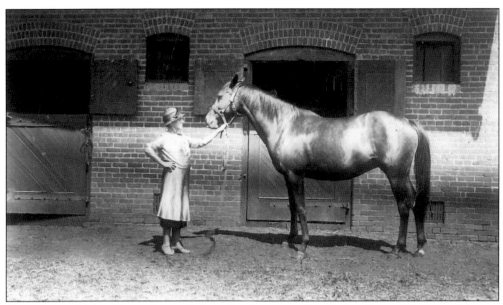

Governor and Mrs. Davis show off their fine horses at Big Spring Farm. (Courtesy Morven Park Archives.)

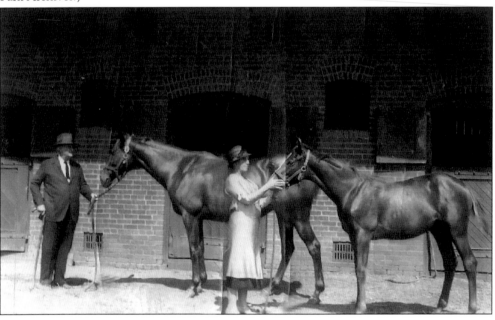

This is a snapshot of a thoroughbred yearling filly owned by Governor Davis that won a first-place ribbon at the Middleburg Horse Show. (Photo by T.N. Darling of Middleburg, Virginia; courtesy Morven Park Archives.)

The Davises loved all equestrian sports. Here, one of their harness racers is being put through his paces. (Courtesy Morven Park Archives.)

Mrs. Davis was as much at home in her carriage with her dog at her side as she was on horseback. This photo was taken during a ride at Tuxedo Park. The Davises traveled extensively and were well known in all the equestrian circles. (Courtesy Morven Park Archives.)

Mrs. Davis enjoys herself at the reins of a four-horse dogcart at Morven Park. (Courtesy Morven Park Archives.)

This is a portrait of Governor Davis in his "hunting pinques" at his estate. According to research, "Pinques" was actually the name of a tailor who created elaborate hunting costumes. Governor Davis participated in many events related to fox hunting not only at his estate, but also up and down the east coast. His hunt breakfasts and balls were legendary in Northern Virginia, Maryland, and Pennsylvania. The portrait was painted by Percy Wilde. (Author photo.)

Governor Davis readies for an early fox hunt at Morven Park. In this photo, he inspects his pack of hounds just before the hunt begins. (Courtesy Morven Park Archives.)

Marguerite Davis is riding a noble steed fully groomed and ready for action. (Courtesy Morven Park Archives.)

Today, Morven Park remains a beautiful estate. The mansion, with its beautiful tapestries, fine china, exquisite furnishings, trophy room, and beautiful gardens, attracts thousands of visitors each year. Here you can see the beauty of a bygone era forever preserved by the Westmoreland Davis Memorial Foundation Inc. (Courtesy Morven Park Archives.)

The mansion at Morven Park has had many additions over the years and has been host to many of Virginia's finest equestrians and sportsman. This photo shows how the mansion looked after renovations by Governor Davis. It is easy to understand why Morven Park has been a favored hunting ground through the years.

One of the more ambitious undertakings by Morven Park was commenced in 1980 with the establishment of the Marion duPont Equine Medical Center. The center is located on 200 acres of the estate and is one of the finest equine medical facilities in the world.

Two

THE MUSEUM OF HOUNDS AND HUNTING

The mansion at Morven Park has several rooms set aside to honor the huntsmen and the hounds. Established in 1985, the museum features the hunting memorabilia of Gov. Westmoreland Davis and his colleagues.

In 1997, a portion of the museum was dedicated as the "Huntsman's Room." This is a tribute to past huntsmen held in high regard by their peers and those who made outstanding contributions to the sport of hunting. This collection is located in several rooms of the mansion. It contains beautifully displayed art works, photographs, and memorabilia from some of the most noted equestrians in the United States. This museum is open to the public on a limited basis.

This sign hangs at the entrance of the Museum of Hounds and Hunting at Morven Park.

This beautiful statue is a memorial to Harry Worcester Smith and his horse, Strongbow. It is one of the focal points in the Museum of Hounds and Hunting. H.W. Smith was Master of the Foxhounds (M.F.H.) and a grand huntsman of Grafton Hunt in Maine. Other huntsmen represented as of 1997 included Thomas Allison, New York; Hunton F. Atwell, M.F.H., Loudoun County, Virginia Hunt; Charles Carver, Virginia; Elias Chadwell, Middlebrook Hunt, New York; Homer B. Gray, New York; A. Henry Higginson, M.F.H., Middlesex, Maine; Mason Houghland, M.F.H., Hillsboro, Tennessee; Sterling Leach, Orange County, Virginia Hunt; Dallas Leith, Elkridge Harford Hunt, Maryland; Robert Maddox, Middleburg Hunt, Virginia; Charles Smith, Pennsylvania; William P. Wadsworth, M.F.H., New York; and William Woodward of Quebec, Canada. (Author Photo.)

This photograph shows one of the many displays in the museum. It contains memorabilia of each of the huntsmen honored along with interesting paintings and photographs from different hunts. The museum also includes a wonderful display of vintage clothing as well as photos of Jacquelyn Kennedy in her riding habit and in action with various hunts. (Author Photo.)

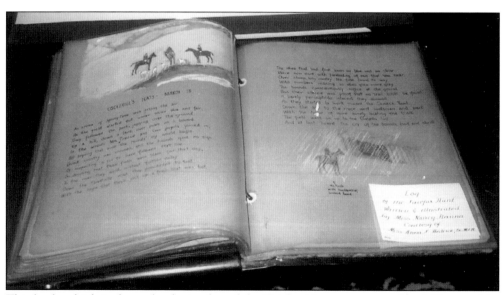

This book, which is the author/artists log of the Fairfax Hunt, was created and illustrated by Nancy Hannah. It was given to the museum by Miss Anna Hedrick, M.F.H., who lived at the Fruitland Estate near Taylorstown in Loudoun County, Virginia.

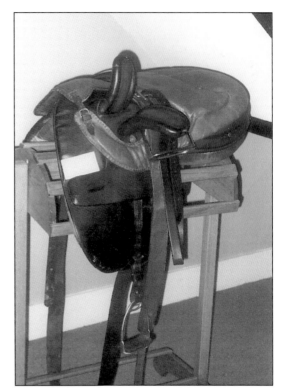

This display shows two distinct styles of saddles, the side-saddle and a version of an English saddle. The Winmill Carriage Collection and the mansion house at Morven Park have vast collections of harnesses, saddles, and carriages that tell the story of bygone eras. Visitors can see saddles that were owned by the rich and famous!

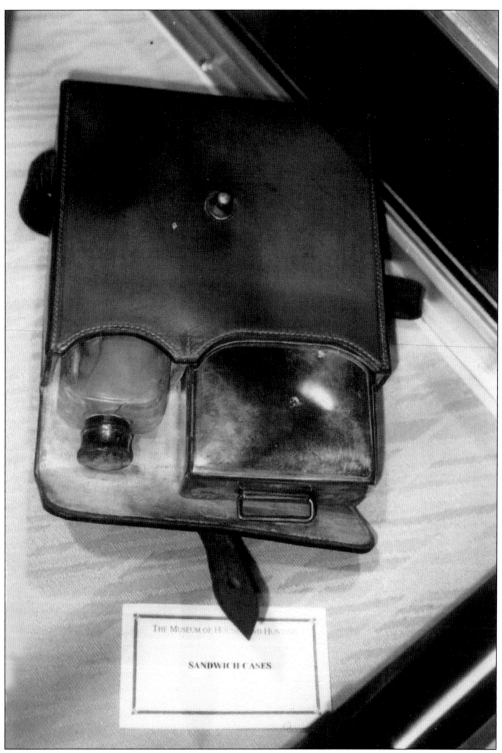

THE MUSEUM OF HUNTING AND HUNTING

SANDWICH CASES

One of the more interesting displays is a leather sandwich case carried by Governor Davis while he was in the field.

Three

THE WINMILL
CARRIAGE COLLECTION

Robert C. and Viola Townsend Winmill dominated the field of equestrian sports. They lived in Warrenton, Virginia for over 50 years, where they played polo, raced horses, raised hounds, and drove and collected coaches. Viola T. Winmill (1891–1975) was well established as a breeder of hounds, a master coachman, and was one of the "first ladies" of fox hunting. In March 1969, Morven Park broke ground for the Winmill Carriage Museum, the home for Mrs. Winmill's vast collection of carriages. A lovely portrait of Viola Townsend Winmill (c. 1939) greets visitors as they enter the carriage house at Morven Park.

This photo is of Viola T. Winmill on her farm, Clovelly, near Warrenton, Virginia. The hounds are being inspected just before a hunt. (Courtesy Morven Park Archives.)

The early winter is a wonderful time for riding in the hunt country of Northern Virginia. This photo shows Viola T. Winmill, M.F.H., and John Mason McClanahan on the horses Rain Hawk and Grey Bird. The hounds are ready for the hunt. (Courtesy Morven Park Archives.)

This is a photo of Robert Winmill on his horse, Gypsy Queen, and Viola T. Winmill on her new mare, Royal Rose, at a meet at the estate of Creedmore in 1925.

Viola Winmill, M.F.H. (left) and Miss Charlotte Noland, M.F.H. (right) are pictured here riding their horses, Gliding Princess and Winterweather. Miss Noland, a noted horsewoman and Master of the Foxhounds of Middleburg Hunt from 1932 to 1946, was founder of Fox Croft School in Middleburg, Virginia in 1914. Notice the ladies ride sidesaddle. (Courtesy Morven Park Archives.)

Viola T. Winmill made a coach tour before the Virginia Gold Cup Races in 1931. Mrs. Winmill, at the reins, made three trips that day from the estate of North Wales in Fauquier County to her estate, Clovelly, near Warrenton, proving her prowess as a coachwoman. The passengers were Mr. and Mrs. Baltazzi, Mrs. Fox, Mrs. Johnston, Mrs. Fowler, Mrs. Norton, and Mr. Fowler. (Courtesy the Winmill Collection, Morven Park.)

Here Mrs. Winmill is shown at the reins of an elaborate six-horse team. Viola loved giving tours and showing off the Northern Virginia countryside. (Courtesy the Carriage House Collection, Morven Park.)

Mrs. Viola T. Winmill arrives at a meet in her open carriage. She enjoyed meeting with the younger equestrians and encouraged them to experience all of the flavor of the horse world. (Courtesy the Winmill Collection, Morven Park.)

Viola Winmill, a nationally known equestrian, was contacted in December 1952 by Wells Fargo and Company of California to help find a horse and driver for the Wells Fargo stagecoach to be used in the inaugural parade of President Eisenhower. The stagecoach, to be driven by a Washington-area driver, was to represent the home state of Vice President Richard M. Nixon. Mrs. Winmill, who was chosen to drive the stagecoach, is seen here in the inaugural parade. The photo was autographed and given to Mrs. Winmill by President Eisenhower. (Courtesy the Carriage House Collection, Morven Park.)

Viola T. Winmill traveled extensively and was willing to try new and interesting adventures. In the 1930s, she met her husband at the Mill Neck Station in New York leading a zebra. The Winmills then walked from the station to the Kerr House (with the zebra) for an entertaining evening. Nederu, the zebra, would become a large part of the Winmills' life at Clovelly. Mrs. Winmill bought a zebra coat and had a room of her house designed in a zebra motif. This photo shows Nederu pulling a pony cart with Viola at the reins after extensive training.

The horse-drawn hearse that carried the body of Viola Winmill to its final resting place in Warrenton Cemetery, where hundreds of mourners attended her funeral, can be seen in the Winmill Collection at Morven Park. Mrs. Winmill lead an interesting life, enjoying herself to the fullest degree, always knowing that women were just as good as men in the field of equestrian sports. Her daughter, Virginia Winmill Livingston Armstrong, wrote a book on her mother's life entitled *Gone Away with the Winmills*.

Four

THE CHRONICLE OF
THE HORSE

In continuous publication since its founding, The Chronicle Of The Horse, *located in Middleburg,*
Virginia, has a vast photographic archive—dating from its beginning in the 1930s—that includes photos
taken by some of the world's most noted sports photographers. The masthead for the magazine reads
"The Chronicle of the Horse is the nation's only source of current news and results for the entire
sport horse community," and the magazine is located in a new building on the same property as the
National Sporting Library.

The photos in this chapter, culled from the tremendous collection of The Chronicle of the Horse,
date from 1948 to 1960. Included are races, jumps, Olympic equestrian events, people, jockeys,
trophies, and much more. In the following pages, readers will see just a fraction of some of the best
equine photos ever taken. All photographs in this chapter are from The Chronicle of the Horse
archives unless otherwise noted.

PENNSYLVANIA NATIONAL; ABIC/USDF REGION 3 and 7 CHAMPIONSHIPS;
BREEDERS' CUP STEEPLECHASE and INTERNATIONAL GOLD CUP

THE CHRONICLE of the Horse

BREEDING • DRESSAGE • HUNTING • SPORT WITH HORSE AND HOUND • SHOWING • CHASING • EVENTING

VOL. LXIV, NO. 44   FRIDAY, NOVEMBER 2, 2001

$52.00 Per Year
$72.00 Per Year Foreign
Single Copy: $2.95

Approaching The Finish At Far Hills

D. Haskell Chhuy

Courtesy of The Byrne Gallery   *Details on Page 70*

This cover of *The Chronicle of the Horse* shows a new style for the publication. There is more art work, but the masthead remains much the same.

History is a large part of *The Chronicle's* collection. Pictured here is Col. "Bill" Drake on King High in 1940. The combination of Colonel Drake and King High would have been a certain bet for the 1940 Olympic games had they been held. Colonel Drake was killed in the Philippines while leading the 8th Cavalry, First Calvary Division.

The Chronicle has photographs taken by some of the best photographers in history. This rare photo shows Col. C.W.A. Raguse on the horse, Trailoka, at the three-day cross-country event in the 1936 Olympic games.

The magazine has many interesting photos that include jockeys from all over the world. This is a photo of some steeplechase jockeys in 1948. Pictured here are A. Morgan, F. Adams, P. Smithwick, J. Schreigner, A. Foote, S. McDonald, and H. Harris. The print and style of the outfits the jockeys wear represent the "stable colors" of the stable for which they ride.

This is the presentation of the Manly Cup Steeplechase, Pimlico, on November 10, 1941. Pictured here, from left to right, are Mrs. Marion duPont Scott, Mrs. W.K. Manly, W.K. Manly Jr., Miss Mathilde Johnston, H.W. Clements, and W.G. Jones (trainer). (Pimlico photo courtesy of *The Chronicle of the Horse*.)

The Chronicle covered worldwide equestrian events of all kinds. This shows some of the Liberty Horses with the Ringling Bros. and Barnum & Bailey Circus in Washington, D.C. in 1952.

In this photo, Madame Luciana is riding a Lippizaner horse in the Ringling Bros. and Barnum & Bailey Circus, c. 1952.

Polo has been a favorite equine sport for many years. *The Chronicle* has an extensive archive of photos showing various matches and clubs. This photo shows Mrs. William D. Fergus presenting trophies to Arlington Farms, winners of the 1948 International Polo League Championship, with seventeen victories and one defeat. Pictured here, from left to right, are Del Carroll, Bill Fergus, Steve Hammond, and Stan Taylor.

This was a dandy day for Cecil Smith and his horse, Texas, in the Easter parade at the Beverly Hills Polo Club *c.* 1948. (Photo by E. Hill courtesy of *The Chronicle of the Horse.*)

These are the United States Open Polo champions in 1959. They are, from left to right, Pedro Silvero, Peter Perkins, George Oliver, and Robert Vihlein Jr.

Polo, a very fast-paced sport, has been a favorite of photographers for many years. This action shot was taken at Meadow Brook showing Robert Skene with Clarence C. Combs on ball in 1952.

Stuart S. Janney was appointed Racing Commissioner of Maryland, *c.* 1948.

The Upperville Horse Show grounds are packed with spectators for the annual horse show in 1948. This photo shows Mr. Kenneth J. Edwards, the owner of the yearling filly winner for that year.

This is one of the photos of trophy presentations in *The Chronicle*'s archives. Here, jockey William Bland Jr. is receiving the Cup from Mrs. Tom Roby, wife of the long-hospitalized jockey in whose honor the race was named and run. At left is Paul Mellon, owner of the Rokeby Stable, in whose colors the horse American Way ran to victory in the first running of the Tom Roby Steeplechase Stakes at Delaware Park. Looking on are Tom Roby's daughters Ellen and Phyllis Ann and trainer Jack Skinner.

This is a photograph of one of the mule races run at the Culpeper Horse Show, c. 1946.

Another view depicts the Culpeper Horse Show grandstand and grounds c. 1947.

At My Lady's Manor Show on August 7, 1948, Master Allen Amos in the saddle of Acres Toy receives the blue ribbon in the Lead Rein Class.

Junior rider Joan Blackwell of Warrenton, Virginia easily clears the jump at Hilldale c. 1948.

"PERSONALLY, I PREFER STRIPES."

Every magazine has to have some humor and *The Chronicle of the Horse* is no exception.

"NO! IT WON'T TURN YOU GREEN! STOP WORRYING ABOUT CHLOROPHYLL!!"

These are some early cartoons that appeared in *The Chronicle*. They were created by a cartoonist named "Trag."

"BET HE'LL MAKE IT THIS TIME."

"WE NEVER SHOULD HAVE TOLD JUNIOR THAT HORSES WERE RELATED TO THE HIPPOPOTAMUS."

Foxhunting is the ultimate equine sport in most of Northern Virginia, Maryland, Pennsylvania, Delaware, and Massachusetts. *The Chronicle* has a full scope of photos of foxhunting in America. Here, Celeste McNeal and her sister Mrs. F.C. McCormack of Brooklandville, Maryland show off their attire, *c.* 1940.

In this photo, taken in old Sudbury, Massachusetts, Millwood Hunt Club Master, Mrs. Henry S. Hull Jr. is followed by Mr. Alex M. Hummer (whipper-in) on the right and Mike Murphy (whipper-in and manager) on the left.

A fox is necessary for a foxhunt and here the Joint Packs meet at Westchester on Christmas day c. 1948. Shown are the H.G. and C.L. Twaddell Hound Packs of Fair Acres at Westtown, Pennsylvania and the I.S. Habersett Pack from Media, Pennsylvania together hunting the fox, which was dropped at Fair Acres. Also shown is Mr. I.S. Habersett, M.F.H., to the left of the cage as his granddaughter, Jean Golf, releases the fox. One of the major differences between British and American foxhunts is that the "Yanks" don't kill the fox. Dropping a fox now is considered bad sportsmanship.

This is a photograph of Hillsboro, Tennessee hounds on a New Year's Day hunt leaving the kennels on Green Pastures, the estate of Mason Houghland, M.F.H. The master is in the foreground with the pack and field following. Many hunts have their own territory along the east coast.

Middleburg, Virginia has long been noted for foxhunting. Here Daniel C. Sands, M.F.H., Miss Charlotte Noland, M.F.H., huntsman R. Maddux, and whipper-in F. Embry discuss the hunt just before the chase begins. Notice the large pack of hounds. This photo was taken c. 1945.

The Middleburg hunt is off with the large pack of hounds in 1948.

The Blue Ridge Hunt is one of the oldest hunts in Virginia. Here they are shown mounting for the hunt—the hounds are ready for the chase. This photo was taken *c.* 1948.

The Orange County Hunt, started in Goshen, New York in 1900 by railroad tycoon E.H. Harriman, has an unusual history. Harriman and his group came to Virginia where they shared the Warrenton hunting country. The Orange County Hunt has included many rich and famous members, including Paul Mellon and Jackie Kennedy. This photo of the Orange County Hunt was taken *c.* 1948.

The Orange Country Hunt of March 1946 included, from left to right, Paul Mellon, Mr. and Mrs. Fredrick Prince Jr., and Mrs. Harold E. Talbott. Notice the ladies are riding sidesaddle.

Breeding and training is very important in foxhounds. Here, at the Bryn Mawr Hound Show, the Orange County Hunt pack, lead by Duke Leach, Huntsman, are put through their paces for the pack class.

Pack classes provide the climax to the annual hound shows. Here the Essex hounds are put to the test. Anderson Fowler, Joint M.F.H., second on the left, keeps a keen eye on the hounds.

Mrs. Lewis Thompson shows her prize-winning basset Stanco Carlton at the Brookdale Basset Show c. 1947.

This cute photo shows Lena's world champion litter of 23 puppies in 1944.

The origin of hunting in Warrenton, Virginia began in colonial times. Hounds owned by Col. Winter Payne (1807–1876) and later by General William H. Payne (Clifton) are given credit with establishing the Bywaters strain of the American hound. Hunting has been a regular sport in Warrenton since 1816. The Warrenton Riding Club was organized in 1873 and the Warrenton Hunt in 1887. The latter was incorporated in 1889 by Messrs. E.P. Astley-Cooper, E.R.W. Baker, James K. Maddux, F.A.B. Portman, and Granville Gaines. This 1948 photo shows several varieties of hounds used in hunting.

Five

THE NATIONAL
SPORTING LIBRARY

The National Sporting Library, located in historic Middleburg, Virginia, was founded in 1954 as a non-profit organization by George Ohrstrom Sr. and author and scholar Alexander MacKay Smith, who served as the curator until his death in 1998.

The library is spectacular inside and outside. The first thing you see in the parking area is a bronze statue of a Civil War Cavalry horse by Tessa Pullan, a gift to the library by the late Paul Mellon. This tribute to the horse—for its loyalty and courage—is magnificent. The plaque on the statue reads: In memory of the one and one half million horses and mules of the Confederate and Union armies who were killed, were wounded, or died from disease in the Civil War. Many perished within 20 miles of Middleburg in the battles of Aldie, Middleburg, and Upperville in June of 1863.

The entrance of the building is admired for its charm, grace, simplistic beauty, and enticing décor. The National Sporting Library collection includes rare first editions, many dating from the 16th century, such as Izaak Walton's The Complete Angler, which is part of the collection of John and Martha Daniels of South Carolina. The library collection also includes drawings by Henry Alken, paintings by Allen Brewer Jr., and books on all facets of equine sports like polo, hunting, riding, jumping, and racing. There are also books on animal breeding, different types of birds and animals, how to train and show horses, and a large amount of information on veterinary medicine.

This bronze statue honoring the over one million horses killed or wounded during the Civil War appears outside of the National Sporting Library.

This sign appears at the entrance to the National Sporting Library.

The National Sporting Library is supported by many lifetime patrons. The beautiful plaque near the entrance lists its famous founding patrons, which are George L. Ohrstrom Jr. of The Ohrstrom Foundation, Forrest E. Mars Sr., Jacqueline B. Mars, John and Martha Daniels, Jane Forbes Clark, Alice duPont Mills, Paul Mellon, Robert H. Smith, and Edward P. Evans.

One can hardly mention sporting art and not include Paul and Rachel Mellon. They completed the Brick House at Oak Spring in Upperville, Virginia in 1941, which contains a gallery of British sporting art. The Mellon family has acquired one of the best collections of sporting art in America and has added much to the National Sporting Library collection. Here is a 1952 photo of Paul and Rachel Mellon accepting one of their many trophies.

Pictured here, from left to right, are Randolph Rouse, M.F.H. Fairfax Hunt; George Ohrstrom Jr., president of the Orange County Hunt; and Arthur "Nick" Arundel in 1975. (Photo by Marshall Hawking.)

The Sporting Library is rich in hunting history and contains a brochure by Swaine Adeney entitled "A Field Guide to Foxhunting," which offers tips for hunters. Some of the tips included are the following: "manners make the man," "promptness is a necessity," "one must allow the hounds, Huntsman, and Masters to go first then it is a free for all," "the Field-masters word is law and should be obeyed to the letter," "the worst sin is to over take the hounds," "the Huntsman must blow his horn before you leave the hunt area," "there is no substitute for hand made leather boots," and "proper and traditional dress for a male must include a red coat although scarlet is an acceptable color." Carter Hall in Clarke County, Virginia has been the scene of many large hunts, some with up to 200 hunters and 50 hounds.

This is a photo of John Dulany, the father of Col. Richard Hunter Dulany. John Dulany, the owner of the estate of Welbourne, would have been surprised to learn that in the late 1800s the estate would become a premiere foxhunting arena in Northern Virginia.

This photo is of Col. Richard H. Dulany of Welbourne, who was in the 7th Virginia Cavalry CSA. His equestrian training must have served him well during the Civil War.

In 1870, Col. Richard Hunter Dulany formed one of the first packs of hounds in the Fauquier County and Upperville areas, which opened up a new and larger hunting area in Northern Virginia.

This is a fascinating 1920s photo of Bentons Gate with the Middleburg Hunt. Mr. and Mrs. Daniel C. Sands are at the gate. The back of the photo reads, "It was among my mothers papers—she was Neville L. Atkinson (Mrs. Thomas Atkinson) who was a close friend of the Sands and granddaughter of Col. Richard H. Dulany of Welbourne."

At the Middleburg hunt on December 29, 1937, Charles Perking Jr. and his hounds are ready for the chase. This would be the last hunt for Middleburg for the year.

This photo of Mrs. Fletcher Harper, Lovie Leith, and Mrs. F.M. Prince Jr. shows the ladies riding sidesaddle.

In her full hunting attire, Mrs. Howard Linn of the Piedmont Hunt urges her horse forward, c. 1935.

Waiting for the Middleburg Hunt to begin in 1941 are Betina J. Ward (Mrs. Newell) and Christopher Greer.

Harry Worcester Smith, Master of the Foxhounds and Grand Huntsman, has his photograph taken in full hunt attire.

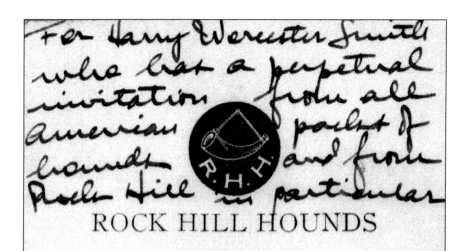

For Harry Worcester Smith who has a perpetual invitation from all american packs of hounds and from Rock Hill in particular

ROCK HILL HOUNDS

Season 1941-42

LT. J. G. RAYMOND R. GUEST, U. S. N.
M. F. H.

ALEXANDER MACKAY SMITH
ACTING M. F. H.

During the season 1941-1942 **hounds** will meet twice a week, generally **on Tues-**days and Fridays with an occasional **bye-**day on Thursdays. The time and **place of** meets may be ascertained by telephoning Boyce 75-J.

Hunting will be by invitation only, and a general invitation to hunt is extended to all owners and renters of land in the Blue Ridge and Rock Hill countries. **During** the Master's absence on naval duty, the hounds will be supported partly by **sub-**scription and by a capping fee for visitors of $15.00 per hunt.

Alexander Mackay Smith

This personal note from Alexander MacKay Smith to Harry Worcester Smith demonstrates their admiration for their hounds and hunts.

Alexander MacKay Smith, a noted equestrian artist, is photographed on one of his many beloved horses, Merry Prince.

The trio of Paul Mellon, Frank Voss, and Harry Worcester Smith was a common sight at hunts all over Northern Virginia. Most people describe Paul Mellon as a generous man who loved art and horses.

In 1957, the Piedmont Hunt was one of the largest in Virginia. Here, the Piedmont Master of Hounds prepares to start the hunt.

Weddings have always been gala events in the hunt country. In this 1960 photo, Newell Ward, Master of the Hounds for Middleburg Hunt, poses with his bride.

Diana Johnson Firestone and her husband, Bertram, were the owners of Catoctin Stud Farm near Waterford in Loudoun County, Virginia in the 1980s and 1990s. There they bred some of the finest racehorses in the United States. Diana Johnson was an accomplished equestrian and this photo shows her taking a jump at the Warrenton Horse Show grounds in Fauquier County in 1960. She was married at that time to Richard Stokes. (Photo by Marshall Hawkins.)

Dr. Joseph M. Rogers of Hamilton, Loudoun County, Virginia rides one of his favorite horses, The King of Spades. This horse, born on his farm in Hamilton, was sired by Cormac and the dam was Salome. (Photo by Marshall Hawkins.)

To the M.F.H. of
Old Persimmond
Hounds with the
Compliments and
regards of the
master of the
middleburg.

Daniel C. Sands poses for a photo. The inscription says, "To the M.F.H. of Old Persimmond Hounds with the compliments and regards of the Master of the Middleburg Hunt."

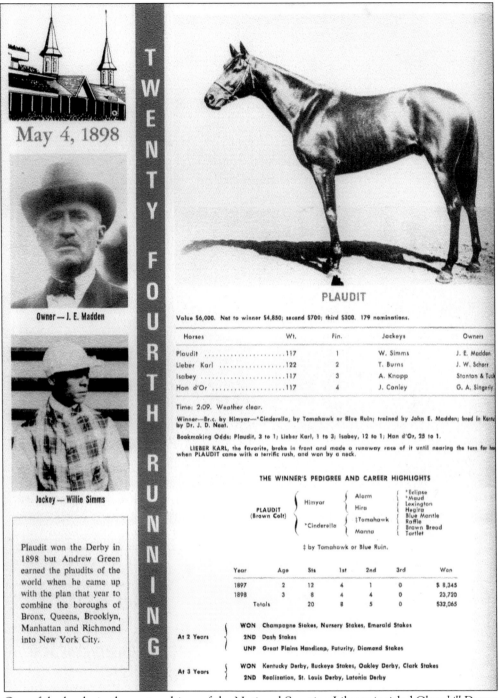

May 4, 1898

Owner — J. E. Madden

Jockey — Willie Simms

T W E N T Y   F O U R T H   R U N N I N G

Plaudit won the Derby in 1898 but Andrew Green earned the plaudits of the world when he came up with the plan that year to combine the boroughs of Bronx, Queens, Brooklyn, Manhattan and Richmond into New York City.

PLAUDIT

Value $6,000. Net to winner $4,850; second $700; third $300. 179 nominations.

Horses	Wt.	Fin.	Jockeys	Owners
Plaudit	117	1	W. Simms	J. E. Madden
Lieber Karl	122	2	T. Burns	J. W. Schorr
Isabey	117	3	A. Knapp	Stanton & Tush
Hon d'Or	117	4	J. Conley	G. A. Singerly

Time: 2:09. Weather clear.

Winner—Br.c. by Himyar—*Cinderella, by Tomahawk or Blue Ruin; trained by John E. Madden; bred in Kentu by Dr. J. D. Neat.

Bookmaking Odds: Plaudit, 3 to 1; Lieber Karl, 1 to 3; Isabey, 12 to 1; Hon d'Or, 25 to 1.

LIEBER KARL, the favorite, broke in front and made a runaway race of it until nearing the turn for ho when PLAUDIT came with a terrific rush, and won by a neck.

THE WINNER'S PEDIGREE AND CAREER HIGHLIGHTS

PLAUDIT (Brown Colt)
- Himyar
  - Alarm
    - *Eclipse
    - *Maud
  - Hira
    - Lexington
    - Hegira
- *Cinderella
  - ‡Tomahawk
    - Blue Mantle
    - Raffle
  - Manna
    - Brown Bread
    - Tartlet

‡ by Tomahawk or Blue Ruin.

Year	Age	Sts	1st	2nd	3rd	Won
1897	2	12	4	1	0	$ 8,345
1898	3	8	4	4	0	23,720
Totals		20	8	5	0	$32,065

At 2 Years
- WON Champagne Stakes, Nursery Stakes, Emerald Stakes
- 2ND Dash Stakes
- UNP Great Plains Handicap, Futurity, Diamond Stakes

At 3 Years
- WON Kentucky Derby, Buckeye Stakes, Oakley Derby, Clark Stakes
- 2ND Realization, St. Louis Derby, Latonia Derby

One of the books in the vast archives of the National Sporting Library is titled *Churchill Downs 100th Kentucky Derby* (courtesy of the Keeneland Library and Phyllis B. Rogers) and contains a photo of jockey Willie Simms, who won the Kentucky Derby twice. In 1898, he rode the winning horse, Plaudit, who was owned by J.E. Madden.

The National Sporting Library has many beautiful paintings both on display and in its archives. There is also a great collection of photos of equine and hunting paintings. This photo, taken of a painting in the Virginia State Library, shows Gen. George Washington and Martha Washington with their huntsman Billy Lee and the two Custis grandchildren. George Washington was a huntsman and enjoyed riding on his estate Mount Vernon.

There are photos of many other animals in the National Sporting Library. This photo shows two fox kits in the wilds of Northern Virginia. The fox has been hunted in America since colonial times. The term foxhunting applies to the red fox, the grey fox, the coyote, or the bobcat—depending on the location of the hunt.

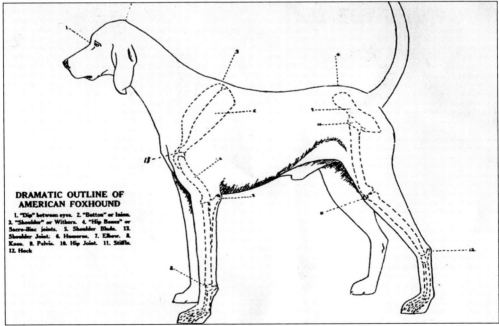

DRAMATIC OUTLINE OF AMERICAN FOXHOUND

1. "Dip" between eyes. 2. "Button" or Inion. 3. "Shoulder" or Withers. 4. "Hip Bones" or Sacro-iliac joints. 5. Shoulder Blade. 12. Shoulder Joint. 6. Humerus. 7. Elbow. 8. Knee. 9. Pelvis. 10. Hip Joint. 11. Stifle. 12. Hock

Hounds play a large part in a foxhunt and many breeds exist in the United States. The Masters of Foxhounds Association of America is the governing body of organized fox, coyote, and drag hunting in the United States and Canada. In 1972, Oatlands Plantation near Leesburg, Virginia was host to a seminar on foxhounds and the American standards for them. This photo was part of drawings showing the basic points of the anatomy of an American foxhound.

69

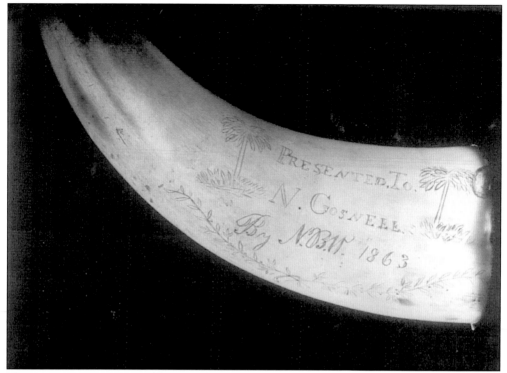

There are many varieties of hunting horns and The National Sporting Library contains the collection of Carlton Smith containing books of music for the horn. This photo shows a hunting horn once owned by Nimrod Gosnell (1820–1884) of Roxbury, Maryland. Napoleon B. Welch of Carroll County, Maryland, presented Gosnell, a famous hound breeder in the 1850s, with the horn. The last owner of this beautiful horn was M.G. Harris of Hancock, Georgia. Collectors value horns of this type.

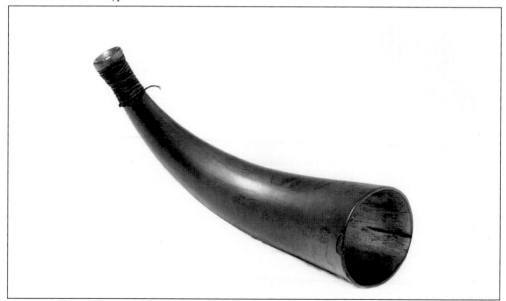

Above is another type of horn used by huntsmen on the east coast.

Six

THE HUNT
MEETS HERE

Northern Virginia has some of the most beautiful estates in the area, and for more than 100 years huntsmen have gathered at these estates to hunt and to socialize. In 1919, Margot Skinner drew a map of the "Tri-Hunting" area and included the top 60 frequented meets in Loudoun, Fauquier, and Prince William Counties. They are as follows: Yellow School House, Philomont, Groveton, Unison, Hibbs Bridge, Llangollen, Blakeley School, Piedmont Kennels, Benton, Pelham's Corner, Welbourne, Homeland, Brookmeade Stables, Rokeby, Chilton, New Ford, Glenwood, Sunny Bank, Exning, Dover, Aldie, Polo Field, Middleburg, Dinwiddie, Atoka, Blue Ridge Stud, J.R. McMann, Glen Ora, Harris Field, Five Points, Whitehouse, Zulla, R.B. Young, McConnell, Grassland, Murray's Gate, White Wood, The Plains, Upperville, Mountville, Clifford, Benton's Bridge, Number 18 School House Road, Ayreshire, Brick House, Fox Croft, Ernest White, St. Brides, Grafton, Lenah, Belray, Mt. Zion, Arcola, Guinea Bridge, Clarks, Redman's, Harper, Rectortown, Phillips, and Russell. This chapter shows you where the huntsmen played, lived, and entertained.

Many of these homes remain in private ownership and continue to allow hunts on their lands. With the vast growth in Northern Virginia, many of these estates are being bought up by developers for country clubs, offices, and subdivisions.

Hillbrook consisted of 670 acres that was granted from Lord Fairfax to John Greg the elder. It is believed that Hamilton Rogers built the original house in the early 1800s, and that Samuel E. Rogers did major renovations and expansions to the original home shortly after the Civil War. Dr. Joseph M. Rogers made some renovations to the house in the 1940s, and he and his wife, Donna Troxell, are active in equestrian circles and continue to allow the hunts to use their property. The house has been in the Rogers family for many generations. Dr. Rogers continues to maintain the house and property as a working farm and stables. This property is listed as a "Bi-Centennial Farm" for the State of Virginia.

This photo shows an earlier view of Hillbrook. The stables have since been expanded and have had extensive preservation work done on them. Hillbrook has changed names over the years but has remained in the Rogers Family. Dr. Joseph M. Rogers has been a respected member of the medical community for many years and has been involved with horses for even longer. He has bred, raised, raced, and ridden horses in the Fox Hunts; he has farmed the land and is an ardent preservationist in Loudoun County; and he has treasured the land and helped preserve the area for future generations to enjoy. Today, Dr. Rogers and his wife enjoy Hillbrook in much the same manner as his father and grandfathers did. He is one of the few true "Virginia gentlemen" left in Loudoun County.

The estate of Rokeby is located near Leesburg, Loudoun County, Virginia. This house, listed on the National Historic Trust Registry, has seen a lot of history. A plaque dedicated in 1994 reads

Rokeby 1757 circa "the (original) records, valuable papers, including Articles of Confederation, the Declaration of Independence, the Constitution of the United States, the correspondence of General Washington, and the Secret Journals of Congress" were stored in the vault at Rokeby August 24, 1814 during the War of 1812. This significant event in the history of the United States of America was verified through research conducted at the United States National Archives by Kathryn I. Coughlan. In 1993, after many years of research, Mrs. Coughlan was able to establish the documentation (Mearns 1952, National Archives 1976) that verifies this event.

This plaque was positioned by the present owners of Rokeby, previous owners, their descendants, and friends of Rokeby.

Mt. Zion Church is located on U.S. Route 50 near Aldie, Loudoun, County, Virginia. Mt. Zion, an old Baptist Church, was the site of a Civil War Battle and has soldiers from both the Northern and Southern armies buried in the graveyard on the property. Mt. Zion was also a place that huntsmen met before hunts for over 100 years. These photos show the church as it looks today. It is being stabilized and restored and is slated to be used for Civil War re-enactments and reunions. It will also serve as a tourist and information center for Loudoun County. (Author photo.)

The estate of Rockland lies on Route 15, just north of Leesburg, Virginia. This gracious old home has been owned by five generations of the Rust family. George Washington Rust bought the land from Burgess Ball and built the main house in about 1822. Hunting in Western Loudoun became more popular after 1900 and the owners of Rockland have hosted meets and allowed hunters to use their land over the years. Not much hunting was done north of Rockland because the land was too close to the Potomac River.

WOODBURN LOUDOUN COUNTY, VIRGINIA

The estate of Woodburn, containing 422 acres, was acquired by George Nixon in the 1740s. The land has had many uses throughout its 250-year history, from farming and livestock to a temporary German POW camp in the 1940s. From the 1890s to the 1950s, Woodburn was one of the prime foxhunt locations in Northern Virginia. The photo above shows the ad for the sale of the property in the 1970s and the photo below is of the mansion itself. (Photo from the John Lewis File, Balch Library.)

OAK HILL

Oak Hill, located on Route 15 just south of Leesburg, Virginia, was the home of President James Monroe. The vast lands of the estate and elegant house have made it a popular place for Northern Virginia Hunts. This drawing shows the house at Oak Hill before additions were made and the gardens established.

Oak Hill is one of the most recognized properties in the state of Virginia. Its plans were drawn up by Thomas Jefferson, and it was constructed under the auspices of Capt. James Hoban, designer and builder of the White House in Washington, D.C. It was home to President James Monroe and is said to be where he drafted the Monroe Doctrine. Lafayette visited there while he was in the United States; evidence of his visit is seen in the form of two chandeliers that he gave as gifts. There are dinosaur footprints in the garden stones; Oak Hill boasts one of the most beautiful gardens in the area. Col. John S. Mosby was entertained there during the Civil War. Coil. John Fairfax, who owned Oak Hill after the Civil War, established it as a nationally known breeding farm for Hackney horses. Many large hunts have used the Oak Hill property since about 1870 and up until about the mid-1930s. This photo shows one of the larger hunts on the lawn at Oak Hill. (Courtesy the Balch Library Archives.)

Belmont was built between 1799 and 1802 by Ludwell Lee, son of Richard Henry Lee, a signer of the Declaration of Independence. This plantation was a refuge for President James Madison when the British burned Washington, D.C. in 1812, and later Lafayette was entertained here. Miss Margaret Mercer, who was opposed to slavery and did much with the Colonization of Liberia for African Americans, had a school here in the early 1800s. In the early 1900s, the 1,200-acre estate was a regular place for many Northern Virginia hunts. The Belmont Races have attracted thousands of spectators over the years. Today a portion of the estate and the mansion house has been turned into a country club with the remainder of the estate being divided and developed. Shown above and below are two views of this marvelous old estate.

Llangollen Farm lies in Upperville, Virginia and consists of over 11,000 acres. Built around 1800 by Col. Levin Powell, Llangollen has long been associated with fast horses and timber races. Llangollen has a rich history and once played host to President Thomas Jefferson. The farm was a gift to Mary Elizabeth Altemus on her marriage to John Hay Whitney, who later became United States Ambassador to Great Britain. Llangollen is best known as a breeding farm for show and race horses. Many Hollywood stars have been guests at Llangollen, including Elizabeth Taylor, Pearl Bailey, Robert Mitchum, and Zsa Zsa Gabor. Today Llangollen is still a working farm and tourist attraction.

Selma was part of a 10,000-acre estate owned by Mrs. Ann Thomson Mason of Gunston Hall. Armstead Thomson Mason built the house between 1800 and 1810. The estate was later owned by United States senator General Mason who was known as "the chief of Selma," and later by the Beverly family. The parents of Mrs. Harry F. Byrd Sr. sold the property to the descendants of the late Gov. Thomas Swann of Morven Park. In 1896, Elijah B. White, of the famed Laurel Brigade of the Civil War, purchased the property. The house was heavily damaged by fire shortly thereafter and then rebuilt. In recent years, Ruth and Ben Epperson owned the property and held weddings and social engagements there. Today the property has been subdivided and the mansion sold with little acreage. Selma is just north of Leesburg, Virginia on U.S. Route 15. (Courtesy the John Lewis File, Balch Library.)

Beacon Hill's tudor-style manor house in 1912, was the home of television and personality Arthur Godfrey from 194? 1979.   PHOTOGRAPHY Courtesy of Long

The estate of Beacon Hill, home of radio and television personality Arthur Godfrey, was the scene of several hunts. Today the estate has been subdivided and is known as Beacon Hill Estates.

Woodgrove has long been a part of the equestrian world. The house, which dates from the mid-1700s, is part of the National Trust. Woodgrove once had its own voting precinct, church, and one-room schoolhouse. Extensive work has been done to the house and some of the outbuildings.

Institute Farm has an interesting history. Originally owned by William Gulick, it is one of the first agricultural institutes in America. Gulick purchased approximately 421 acres from Mr. and Mrs. S.L. Governor. Mrs. Governor, the former Maria H. Monroe, was the daughter of President James Monroe of Oak Hill Plantation just south of Leesburg, Virginia. The Gulicks owned the property until the 1870s. During a battle in the Civil War, which took place on part of the property, 30 people were killed, 66 were wounded, and over 100 prisoners were taken. A monument was erected to commemorate the event on Route 734. Since 1916, the property has belonged to the Institute Corporation and is leased to the National Beagle Club of America. Institute Farm now has 508 acres and is used for many activities of the American Beagle Club, including spring and fall pack trials for beagles and bassets. It is licensed and sanctioned by the American Kennel Club and hosts the specialty show for beagles and the annual Triple Challenge for all types of beagles.

Chestnut Hill was built after 1796 and was originally one room wide, two rooms deep, and two stories high. The house was built on land owned by Josias Clapham, who was one of the original trustees of the towns of Leesburg and Middleburg. His daughter, Betsey, married Thompson Mason of Gunston Hall and the property was known as a "Mason home" until the 1930s. Over the years, many elaborate parties and hunts have been held here.

Woodlea was built about 1835 for Thomas Saunders and remained in the Saunders family until 1917. One of the unique features of this house is the number of closets. There is at least one closet for each room in the house. Today the land has been sold and subdivided with only about 10 acres remaining with the house itself. Woodlea has been the scene of many parties, dinners, and hunts during its 175-year history.

Neptune's Lodge was part of Thomas Lee's tract of land in the 1700s and Gov. William "Extra Billy" Smith built the house c. 1845. James K. Maddux bought the estate about 1895 and changed the name from Monte Rosa to Neptune's Lodge in honor of his famous racehorse.

Burrland, the Training Barn and Espino, one of the farm stallions

Burrland, near Middleburg, was the home of Mr. and Mrs. William Ziegler of New York. Noted for breeding studs as well as hunting, Burrland jockeys wore silks of scarlet and green.

The homes and farms that served the huntsmen bred, raised, and sold horses like the famous polo pony Norah, raised on the farm of Mr. Whitney at his estate near Upperville, Fauquier County, Virginia. Most estates had stables and some boarded horses for weekend rides by huntsmen.

Six

TALLY HO! LOUDOUN

The Civil War devastated the foxhunting lands of Loudoun County and most of the hounds had been let loose to roam the countryside with only a few first rate packs remaining. Nevertheless, with courage and conviction the foxhunters rallied and with the help of the land barons, such as Col. Richard Hunter Dulany and William Ashton, the breeding of hounds once again became paramount. In 1894, Arthur Mason Chichester, William Heflin, and William C. Eustice joined to form the Loudoun County Hunt. The pack was too small for the vast Loudoun County estates so A.H. Higginson invited English hounds from Massachusetts to participate and in 1908, Harry Worcester Smith brought down his Grafton hounds. With these events, foxhunting was once again a thriving sport in Northern Virginia.

Loudoun County has been horse country for almost three centuries and has not only foxhunting events, but also horse shows and races.

With so many large landholders in Loudoun County, the owners became interested in breeding and raising horses to help support the lands and keep the farms intact. It was only natural that fox hunting became a large part of the history of Loudoun County.

Some of the large estates have disappeared over the past 50 years, but determined horse-lovers are keeping Loudoun's equestrian heritage alive.

Dr. Joseph M. Rogers, Master of the Loudoun County Hunt, leads his pack to a hunt as the fog lifts from Morven Park. He is riding Virginia Volunteer and following him are Harry Wight, Vaughn Clatterbuck, Pat Hurrocks, Anita Graff White, Po Oliver, and David Moyes. (Courtesy Dr. J.M. Rogers.)

Getting ready for the 1948 horse
show in Ashburn, Virginia was a
daylong event.

The photographer Winslow Williams identified this photo as follows: The horses are on display and being judged as they prepare for the Blue Ridge Point to Point Races in 1956.

This photo depicts a large Loudoun turnout at the Piedmont Races in 1955. (Courtesy Winslow Williams Collection, Balch Library.)

Middleburg is the best-known town in Loudoun's Hunt Country and has been part of the foxhunting scene for over 200 years. One of the focal points for the hunting set is the Red Fox Inn, one of the oldest taverns in Loudoun County and a social center where huntsmen and tourists often dine. Middleburg has often played a part in the numerous equestrian events that have taken place on the nearby estates that the rich, famous, and infamous have called home. Middleburg has an ambiance that mixes culture and class with everyday life.

These two photos were taken at the Middleburg Races in the 1940s. Everyone seems to be having a good time!

This parade took place in Leesburg, going north on what is now U.S. Route 15 (King Street), in the early 1900s. (Courtesy the Winslow Williams Collection, Balch Library.)

Purcellville became part of the hunt scene sometime after 1900 with mostly riding and jumping sports. This photo was taken at the Purcellville Pony Show in April 1951. (Courtesy Winslow Williams Collection, Balch Library.)

This stud horse, belonging to Mr. Snodgrass, poses with his trainer around 1955. (Courtesy Winslow Williams Collection, Balch Library.)

The estate known as Raspberry Plain had several horse shows. This one, in 1948, drew a large crowd. (Courtesy Winslow Williams Collection, Balch Library.)

Riders like this one attracted a lot of attention at the Raspberry Plain Horse Show in 1948.

OLDEST HORSE SHOW IN THE UNITED STATES

OFFICAL CATALOGUE
UPPERVILLE COLT AND HORSE SHOW
(ORGANIZED 1853)

DARLING PHOTO

ROYALTY II, CHAMPION 1940

To Be Held At

Grafton Farm, Near Upperville, Va.

FRIDAY-SATURDAY, JUNE 13-14, 1941

PRICE TWENTY - FIVE CENTS

The Upperville Horse Show grounds are the oldest in America, with the first colt show taking place in 1852. Col. Richard Hunter Dulany, who lived on the estate Welbourne near Upperville, developed the idea of an annual show. One of the largest land owners in the Blue Ridge and an avid equestrian, he gave silver "Loving Cups" by Lewis C. Tiffany of New York as prizes at his early horse shows. Tiffany was so inspired after speaking with Colonel Dulany about his horse show project that he agreed to make the prizes for only the price of the silver. (Courtesy National Sporting Library.)

Unison, Virginia remains a small village in Loudoun County surrounded by open space. The hunters often met at the store, where the road was lined with cars and horse trailers. (Courtesy Winslow Williams Collection, Balch Library.)

The members of the Loudoun Hunt are off in this 1955 photo. (Courtesy Winslow Williams Collection, Balch Library.)

Many women have ridden with the Loudoun Hunt. This photograph is of Margaret Titus in 1955. (Courtesy Winslow Williams Collection, Balch Library.)

Arthur Godfrey's estate, Beacon Hill, was prime hunting land in Loudoun County. Here Dr. Joseph M. Rogers and Alexander MacKay Smith exchange words of praise after a ride c. 1955. (Photo courtesy Balch Library Archives.)

The hunters of Loudoun have always loved their horses. These photos show the horse cemetery at Notre Dame Academy located near Middleburg, Virginia. The cemetery, which is located in a small grove of trees, contains about eight to ten gravesites devoted to horses. The Carter family cemetery is located in a field about one half mile away.

Middleburg Team *Baltimore Team*

Maryland Polo Club Bests Middleburg At Welbourne Field
By MISS WINIFRED MADDUX

IN the early part of July were played the two match games between the Maryland Polo Club Team from the Green Spring Valley and the Middleburg Team at Welbourne Field, near Middleburg, Virginia.

It was a broiling July day with the usual hard going which is so tough on the ponies; all the summer residents from this sporting Northern Virginia section were much in evidence as well as visitors from Baltimore and Washington.

The lineup for Maryland was Arthur Foster at 1, John Waller Foster at 2, William Martin at 3, and Wallace Lanahan at Back.

The Middleburg lineup was Richard Kirkpatrick at 1, Winston Frost at 2, Baldwin Spilman at 3, and William P. Hulbert (captain) at Back.

Some excellent polo was displayed by that rising young player, Winston Frost. This boy is certainly great polo material if he continues the way he has been playing lately.

The score at the end of the sixth chukker was 5 to 12 in favor of the Maryland team.

The second match game between these two teams was played on the same field a couple of days later; the lineup for Maryland being slightly different, with Clarence Wheelwright playing at 2 instead of J. W. Foster. The Middleburg lineup was almost entirely changed, Winston Frost alone keeping his original position. The other players were Henry Frost, Dr. A. C. Randolph, and Charles Sabin. In this game the first goal was made by Martin of the Maryland Team. Some beautiful shots were made by Lanahan, and Winston Frost played a splendid game.

This game unfortunately was stopped before the end on account of the heavy downpour of rain which made playing impossible.

The score when both teams stopped playing was 6 to 2 in favor of the Maryland team.

Major Cunningham   Dick Kirkpatrick   Baldwin Spilman   Lieutenant Noble   Jock Whitney

Photo by Courtesy of The Baltimore Sun

As Loudoun-Fauquier Defeated Third Cavalry at Polo, June 14, 1931, at Stephenson, Virginia

Polo has been and still is a favorite sport of many equestrians as this page from the 1932 *Loudoun-Fauquier Breeders Magazine* shows.

After World War II, Rokeby Estate, near Leesburg, offered coach rides on Sunday afternoon on U.S. Route 15. The heavy traffic of today would make this type of entertainment impossible.

The *Loudoun Times Mirror* has been the local newspaper for Loudoun County in one title or another since the 1790s. One of the more interesting features is "Out of the Attic," which is the latest title of the column that has run in the paper since the 1870s. In later years, Miss Frances Reid, the author of the column, added photos from various sources, which not only enhanced the paper, but also gave readers a glimpse of the past. Many people, including historians and genealogists, have benefited from this column. Arthur Arundell, the publisher of the *Loudoun Times Mirror*, has given his collection of early editions of the paper to the Thomas Balch Library. Also contained in the collection are some of the newspaper's predecessors including one called *The Genius of Liberty* in the early 1800s. The following "Out of the Attic" photos show the importance of the horse in Loudoun County's history.

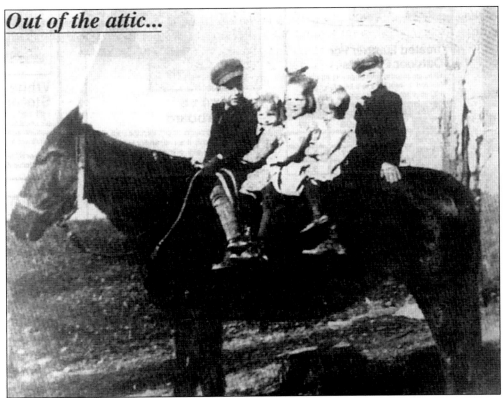

These are the Walter Hough children of Middletown, seen in a photograph taken by Mildred Orrison in 1910. They are, from left to right, Vance, Doris, Susie, Loretta, and Harry. Catherin, the oldest of the Hough children, was absent when the picture was taken. All are now living in Virginia and are over the age of 80 years.

Robert Flynn of Leesburg, the caretaker at Morven Park in the days of Westmoreland Davis, takes children for a ride in one of the vehicles from Morven Park's carriage collection. The boy in the front seat is Lawrence Glodstone. In the back seat are Michael Ramos, left, and Robie Simpson, right. Dottie Galdstone, the former administrative assistant at Morven Park, loaned the picture to the *Times-Mirror*. Jim Birchfield, a former *Times-Mirror* editor, took the picture.

Riders and hounds are ready to take off from the Red Apple, Leesburg, January 1949. Dr. Joe Rodgers, left, is seen aboard Lord Loudoun; John Paul rides Tulmore Bob and Hunton Atwell is aboard War Veteran. Atwell was the huntsman that year, and Paul and Rogers were whippers-in.

As Loudoun's 4-Hers prepare to celebrate the Golden Anniversary of the 4-H Fair August 6-10, one photo entry from that first 4-H Fair is happily discovered. This oxen-drawn covered wagon, loaned by Nina Carter Tabb of Middleburg, was a highlight in the parade on Purcellville Fairgrounds that September 1936. J.R. Lintner was county extension agent that year. William H. Cockerill was the assistant agent and Karl Bundy was the home agent.

The *Times-Mirror's* quest for old photographs, reminiscent of bygone days, has brought in entertaining photography. Holmes Gregg of Lincoln recalls the thrilling sight and sound of bells on the six-horse team, the property of the late Thomas Janney Brown of "Circleville" whose farm was between Lincoln and North Fork and is still in the family. The grain-loaded wagon from "Circleville" is approaching the Purcellville mill. Note the "Pancoast and Paxson" sign on the building at right. Clayton Polen stands by the wagon; the identity of the rider is unknown. The photo was made by the late Bentley Gree more than 60 years ago.

Mules, Jack and Jim, with driver John Smith, make a delivery of feed to the C.C. Shaffer Mill at Leesburg in the 1930s. According to "Clint" Shaffer, the mules were washed down the Potomac River in a flood, ending up at the Shaffer Mill without anyone knowing who the owners were. Smith plowed gardens around Leesburg and delivered feed to the mill with the help of the mules.

Equestrian events attract crowds of all ages. Here, Lowell Riley enjoys the Loudoun Hunt events in 1955. (Courtesy Winslow Williams Collection, Balch Library.)

Informal riding still remains a favorite pastime for many Loudouners. This photo is of P.A. Benedum out for a ride in the 1950s. (Courtesy Winslow Williams Collection, Balch Library.)

Equestrian events often gave junior huntsman and novice riders a chance to show their skills at training and riding horses and ponies. (Courtesy Winslow Williams Collection, Balch Library.)

Miss Anna Hedrick, M.F.H and long-time attorney in Loudoun County, was an avid equestrian. She owned an estate called Fruitland near Taylorstown, Loudoun County, Virginia. These photos, taken in the 1940s or 1950s, are of one of the many hunt socials held there. (Courtesy Winslow Williams Collection, Balch Library.)

Ferriers are a popular and necessary part of most meets, especially large ones. Many ferriers are mobile and not only shoe horses, but also can repair barn door hinges, harnesses, and other types of equipment.

A.V. Symington takes her horse, Red, out for a meet at Arthur Godfrey's estate, Beacon Hill. Godfrey had some of the finest stables in Northern Virginia and hunt meets were frequently held at Beacon Hill in the 1940s and 1950s.

Arthur Godfrey, an accomplished radio and television personality, lived in Loudoun County for many years and often televised his show from Beacon Hill. Godfrey loved to show off his horses and equestrian style. These photos were taken by Winslow Williams as promotional shots.

Arthur Godfrey prepares for a ride in front of his Beacon Hill stables.

Bluemont lies in western Loudoun County and was known as Snickersville for almost 100 years. In this 1880s photo, Roger Glascock stands in front of his horse and buggy on Main Street. Osbourne Stone is standing behind the wagon and Miss Molly Weadon's boarding house can be seen just up the street. Horses were an important form of transportation in Loudoun County until the 1920s.

William Carter Heflin, owner of Rock Hill Farm, Lucketts, Virginia, is shown with his horse, Queen of Diamonds, who was the winner of the Jumper Class at Madison Square Gardens in 1909. Mr. Heflin was the first Master of the Hunt in Loudoun, and his Keevy Beagles Hounds, brought from Ireland, gave the fox a merry chase. This photo was taken at the Loudoun Hunt Club, a red brick building at Market and Church Streets in Leesburg. (Courtesy Cora Heflin Kohloss.)

The three sons of John Robert Heflin of Warrenton, Virginia, came to Loudoun County in the mid-1800s to find their fortunes. William Carter (seated), known as "Buffalo Bill," bought Rock Hill Farm near Lucketts, Virginia. His interests were horses, hunting, and farming. It is said that Col. J.S. Mosby always got a good change of horses from Mr. Heflin whenever he came by during his campaign in the Civil War. John Chilton, with hand on hip, had general stores at Sycolin and Woodburn. Brown Walter, the other man pictured, went into the transportation business in Washington, D.C. (Courtesy Cora Heflin Kohloss.)

This photo, dated December 28, 1948, shows the Loudoun Junior Hunt out for a morning ride. Unfortunately, no one in the picture is identified.

In the mid-1960s, hunts were as popular as ever. This photo shows Su Su Shoemaker Dale (left) and B.J. Webb (right) at Belmont Estate hunting with the Fairfax Hunt. (Courtesy B.J. Webb.)

This photo is of B.J. Webb, who remains an active equestrian in a more limited capacity, taking a jump at the Bull Run Hunt in the autumn of 1978. Ms. Webb is currently the mayor of Leesburg, the seat of a rapidly growing county.

Trevor Hill (Rosemont) is a beautiful 300-acre estate and was the home of Sanford Ramey in the early 1800s. The farm remained in the Ramey family until 1863 when it was sold to Charles Fenton Fadely. The farm remained in the Fadely family until it was recently sold and subdivided. Only a small tract of land remains with the manor house today. Having an eight-box stall stable, a large pond, and lots of open space made Trevor Hill a popular hunting spot until it was subdivided in the 1980s.

Burgess Ball, a cousin of George Washington, purchased the property known as Springwood in 1795 and lavishly entertained there. During the Civil War, Gen. Robert E. Lee held a military conference in the dining room, and in the 1860s, Mr. and Mrs. G.W. Ball ran the Springwood Select Home School for Young Ladies on the property. The school was for young ladies 10 to 16 years of age. Springwood has been the site of many hunts and on occasion, large meets. Springwood is now called Piedmont and is a psychiatric center.

In 1937, the *Loudoun-Fauquier Breeders Magazine* recognized the following Hunt Clubs in Northern Virginia: The Blue Ridge Hunt, Boyce, The Casanova Hunt, The Cobbler Hunt of Deleplane, The Loudoun Hunt, Leesburg, The Middleburg Hunt, Orange County Hunt, Piedmont Fox Hounds, and the Warrenton Hunt. Overall, 60 hunts were recognized in 6 states. It seems that Warrenton Hunt had the only female M.F.H., Mrs. Robert C. Winmill. This page, from the *Loudoun-Fauquier Breeders Magazine* shows snapshots of the Middleburg Hunt Races taken by the *Washington Sunday Star*.

ACKNOWLEDGMENTS

I would like to take this opportunity to thank all of those whose help and support went into the pages of this book. I am grateful to Lee Catlett for her time, patience, and the amazing number of photos she copied for me. I want to thank John Strassburger, publisher of *The Chronicle of the Horse,* and his staff for their patience and for allowing me to use such wonderful photos. I am grateful to The National Sporting Library, Lisa Campbell, and Robert Webber for their patience and photos from their archives. I want to thank John Fishback for data entry and support of my whims, and Phyllis Ford for allowing me to run rampant in the Balch photo archives.

I would also like to thank Tracy Gillespie, director of Curatorial Operations of the Westmoreland Davis Foundation, for technical support and her belief in the book, Lee Heuer for her time and energy in sharing the Winmill Carriage Collection history with me, John Lewis for the use of his historic homes photos, and Morven Park for allowing the use of their photos. I want to thank Will O'Keefe, who is executive director of the Westmoreland Davis Foundation; Dr. Joseph M. and Donna Troxell Rogers for their equestrian expertise, photos, and friendship; and Jane Sullivan, the Thomas Balch Library manager, whose patience and generosity are greatly appreciated. I wish to thank Melissa York for her sense of style and humor and Phillis B. Rogers, the Associate Librarian at Keeneland Library in Lexington, Kentucky for the use of the Willie Simms photos. Thanks to Shenandoah Photographics Inc. for the cover reproduction.

A very special thanks goes out to all the photographers, over the years, whose work has helped keep equestrian history alive.